TURNING POINTS

THE WAR IN IRAQ

BY VALERIE BODDEN

CREATIVE EDUCATION • CREATIVE PAPERBACKS

Published by Creative Education and Creative Paperbacks
P.O. Box 227, Mankato, Minnesota 56002
Creative Education and Creative Paperbacks are imprints of
The Creative Company
www.thecreativecompany.us

Design by The Design Lab
Production by Colin O'Dea
Art direction by Rita Marshall
Printed in China

Photographs by 123RF (VASILIS VERVERIDIS), Alamy (Yaser Jawad/
Xinhua, Laperruque, Trinity Mirror/Mirrorpix, National Geographic Image
Collection), Creative Commons Wikimedia (Richard Block/Flickr, GYSGT
ERIK S. HANSEN/DoD Media, Kimberlee Hewitt/The White House, Islam
Badr, Joshuashearn, CHIEF JOURNALIST S.A. THORNBLOOM/DIMOC, US
Army photo, US DoD Photo, United States Marine Corps/DVIDS, Sgt. Brad
Willeford/U.S. Army photo/DVIDS), Getty Images (PATRICK BAZ/AFP, Yuri
Cortez/AFP, Getty Images/Getty Images News), iStockphoto (3D_generator,
DancingMan, KaninRoman, LeeCraker, roibu, Romanista)

Library of Congress Cataloging-in-Publication Data
Names: Bodden, Valerie, author.
Title: The war in Iraq / Valerie Bodden.
Series: Turning points.
Includes bibliographical references and index.
Summary: A historical account of Operation Iraqi Freedom, including the events
leading up to the 2002 conflict, the people involved, the political instability and
insurgency that arose, and the lingering aftermath.
Identifiers: ISBN 978-1-64026-177-8 (hardcover) / ISBN 978-1-62832-740-3
(pbk) / ISBN 978-1-64000-295-1 (eBook)
This title has been submitted for CIP processing under LCCN 2019935432.

CCSS: RI.5.1, 2, 3, 8; RI. 6.1, 2, 4, 7; RH.6–8.3, 4, 5, 6, 7, 8

First Edition HC 9 8 7 6 5 4 3 2 1
First Edition PBK 9 8 7 6 5 4 3 2 1

TABLE *of* CONTENTS

The president's stance on preemptive action was in opposition to the United Nations' approach regarding military action—yet the U.S. proceeded with Bush's plan.

On January 29, 2002, president George W. Bush delivered the annual State of the Union address. The speech came almost five months after the devastating terrorist attacks of September 11, 2001. Now, the president said, the United States had to defend itself from terrorists and from countries that threatened America. Bush included Iraq, North Korea, and Iran among these countries, calling them an "Axis of Evil." Bush contended that Iraq had been developing weapons of mass destruction, including chemical, biological, and nuclear weapons. He promised the nation, "The United States of America will not permit the world's most dangerous **regimes** to threaten us with the world's most destructive weapons."

Fourteen months later, the U.S. launched Operation Iraqi Freedom. This **preemptive** war was intended to destroy Iraq's weapons of mass destruction. In only three weeks, U.S. forces toppled the regime of Iraqi **dictator** Saddam Hussein. But instead of peace, Iraq descended into chaos. The U.S. soon found itself fighting a growing insurgency and the rise of new terror groups. Meanwhile, inspectors from the United Nations (UN) failed to find weapons of mass destruction in Iraq. Controversy raged over whether the U.S. had been misled into war. More than 15 years after the war began, the outcome of this turning point for Iraq, the Middle East, and the world remained uncertain.

As a country, Iraq is still dependent on its oil; the UN estimates that oil production and exports account for 99 percent of the country's revenue.

CHAPTER ONE

RISING CONFLICT

Operation Iraqi Freedom wasn't the first war between Iraq and the U.S. In 1990, Saddam Hussein accused neighboring Kuwait of illegally drilling for Iraqi oil. In August 1990, the Iraqi army invaded Kuwait. Hussein declared Kuwait was now part of Iraq. This move worried officials in the U.S. and other Western countries. With Kuwait under his control, Hussein held nearly 10 percent of the world's oil supply. From Kuwait, he could also invade Saudi Arabia, which had the largest oil reserves in the world. If Hussein controlled that much of the world's oil supply, he could also control oil prices and availability.

The UN ordered Iraq to withdraw from Kuwait. But Iraq refused. So a coalition of more than 700,000 troops from 28 countries amassed in the Persian Gulf region. On January 16, 1991, president George H. W. Bush announced that the U.S.-led coalition was launching Operation Desert Storm. Six weeks of airstrikes followed by less than a week of ground attacks brought quick victory to the coalition.

Saddam Hussein

Although missiles are often a typical part of a country's armament, Iraq's weapons program was heavily scrutinized in the 1990s.

Many in the U.S. expected Iraq's defeat to lead to Hussein's overthrow by his own people. The **Shiite** majority living in the southern part of Iraq launched a rebellion. So did the **Kurds**, in northern Iraq. However, the rebellions were quickly suppressed by the Republican Guard, an army of 50,000 soldiers loyal to Hussein.

Although Hussein retained power, the U.S. established no-fly zones over northern and southern Iraq to protect the Kurds and Shiites there. In addition, UN **sanctions** prevented Iraq from selling oil. The UN also ordered Iraq to destroy its weapons of mass destruction. Hussein was known to have such weapons, since he had launched chemical attacks against Iranian troops during the Iran-Iraq War of the 1980s. He'd even used these weapons against the Kurds in his own country, killing up to 100,000. To ensure that Iraq got rid of all its weapons of mass destruction, the UN required the country to submit to regular weapons inspections.

Although Iraq allowed UN inspectors into the country, Hussein refused to give them access to many sites. Even so, inspectors managed to find and destroy development sites for nuclear weapons. They also eliminated 38,500 chemical warheads and thousands of gallons' worth of chemical agents.

In August 1998, Iraq declared all its weapons of mass destruction had been eliminated. The country refused to comply with further inspections. In response, the U.S. and Great Britain launched

POINTING OUT

FROM ALLIES TO ENEMIES

By the 1970s, the U.S. purchased $10 billion worth of oil from Iraq every year. When war broke out between Iraq and Iran in 1980, U.S. officials worried that an Iranian victory would be devastating to the West. Iran's leader, Ayatollah Ruhollah Khomeini, had strong anti-Western views. So the U.S. secretly provided aid to Iraq in the form of satellite imagery and weapons sold by U.S. allies. According to some reports, U.S. companies also sold the Iraqis chemicals for making chemical weapons. When the war finally ended without a clear victor in 1988, both sides were significantly weakened. Soon afterward, Iraq kicked U.S. officials out of the country.

Operation Desert Fox. Over the span of 4 days, the joint forces bombed nearly 100 sites in Iraq that inspectors had been unable to access. For the next four years, no weapons inspectors were allowed into Iraq. Many U.S. intelligence officials worried that Iraq was using this time to rebuild its weapons program.

Meanwhile, the U.S. faced other threats. On September 11, 2001, terrorists crashed hijacked planes into the World Trade Center in New York, the Pentagon in Washington, D.C., and a field in Shanksville, Pennsylvania. Nearly 3,000 Americans lost their lives in the attacks. American intelligence officials quickly traced the attacks to **al Qaeda**, headed by Osama bin Laden. But some government officials wondered if there might be any connection to Iraq. "It was too sophisticated and complicated an operation for a terrorist group to have pulled off by itself, without a state sponsor," asserted Paul Wolfowitz, deputy secretary of defense. "Iraq must have been helping them." Some officials began to press for war with Iraq. Others, such as counterterrorism adviser Richard Clarke, felt such a move would be counterproductive. "Having been attacked by al Qaeda," said Clarke, "for us now to go bombing Iraq in response would be like our invading Mexico after the Japanese attacked us at Pearl Harbor."

In the wake of 9/11, Bush declared a widespread "War on Terror." The first focus of this war was Afghanistan's **Taliban**, which had taken control of the government. The Taliban was believed to be providing shelter to bin Laden. After U.S. forces quickly overthrew the Taliban (but bin Laden was still at large), many in the Bush administration turned to making a case for war against Iraq. Among the reasons given for entering a new war in Iraq was the idea that Hussein's brutal regime posed a threat to his own people as well as to his neighbors in the

Osama bin Laden

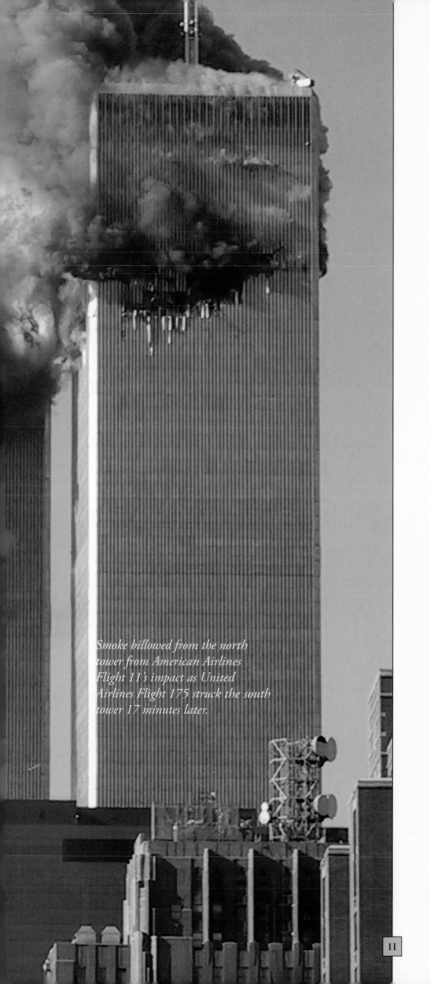

Smoke billowed from the north tower from American Airlines Flight 11's impact as United Airlines Flight 175 struck the south tower 17 minutes later.

Middle East. In addition, Iraqi attacks against U.S. jets patrolling the no-fly zones in northern and southern Iraq had become more frequent.

The administration's primary case for war was its belief in Iraq's weapons of mass destruction capabilities. Some U.S. intelligence officials believed Hussein had thousands of gallons of anthrax. They thought he had enough chemicals to produce 200 tons (181 t) of deadly VX gas. Some intelligence reports indicated Iraq might be developing **drones** to spray chemical or biological weapons over the U.S. Other evidence pointed to Iraq's purchase of aluminum tubes, which might indicate a use of

POINTING OUT

BIRTH OF A DICTATOR

*Saddam Hussein was born April 28, 1937, to a poor family in a village near Tikrit, Iraq. As a boy, he moved to Baghdad. At the age of 20, he joined the relatively small **Baath Party**, which promoted Arab unity. Two years later, he participated in an unsuccessful attempt to assassinate Iraq's president. Afterward, he fled the country but returned when the Baath Party took control in 1963. Saddam quickly rose through the party ranks to become second in command behind General Ahmad Hassan al-Bakr. Saddam became president after al-Bakr's retirement in 1979. Although Iraq's economy prospered under Saddam, the dictator maintained control through threats and violence.*

In 2002, the "boots on the ground" count of U.S. troops in Afghanistan and Iraq totaled only 5,200; this figure jumped to 78,000 with the 2003 invasion.

nuclear **centrifuges**. In addition, some administration officials believed senior members of al Qaeda had been in contact with the Iraqi regime. They feared Hussein might sell his weapons to the terrorists.

In June 2002, Bush announced, "The war on terror will not be won on the defensive. We must take the battle to the enemy, disrupt his plans, and confront the worst threats before they emerge. In the world we have entered, the only path to safety is the path of action." On October 11, Congress authorized Bush to use military force to defend the U.S. against Iraq and to enforce UN Security Council resolutions there. People around the world were divided about engaging in another war with Iraq. As the U.S. edged closer to war, up to 65 percent of Americans polled supported the use of military force to dispel the Iraqi threat. Still, large antiwar protests were held in several major cities across the U.S. and around the world.

In November 2002, the UN ordered Iraq to comply with its earlier resolutions. If it didn't allow inspectors to reenter the country, it would face "serious consequences." Iraq soon agreed. In March 2003, lead UN inspector Hans Blix reported that the new inspections had revealed no evidence of weapons of mass destruction. However, he said Iraq had also not offered its full cooperation in the inspection process.

The U.S. and Britain believed Iraq's lack of cooperation was cause for military action. On March 17, 2003, Bush delivered a televised speech giving the Iraqi dictator an ultimatum: "Saddam Hussein and his sons must leave Iraq within forty-eight hours. Their refusal to do so will result in military conflict commenced at a time of our choosing." To the Iraqi people, he promised, "The tyrant will be gone soon. The day of your liberation is near."

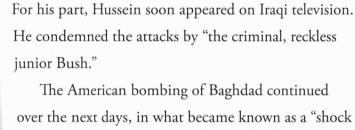

CHAPTER TWO

MILITARY OPERATIONS

O n March 19, 2003, American intelligence indicated that Hussein and other senior Iraqi officials might be gathered at one of his family homes. President Bush ordered an immediate airstrike against the target. Although that intelligence proved to be wrong, the airstrikes officially launched Operation Iraqi Freedom. That night, Bush announced to the American people, "My fellow citizens, at this hour, American and coalition forces are in the early stages of military operations to disarm Iraq, to free the people, and to defend the world from grave danger."

For his part, Hussein soon appeared on Iraqi television. He condemned the attacks by "the criminal, reckless junior Bush."

The American bombing of Baghdad continued over the next days, in what became known as a "shock and awe" campaign. As Lieutenant General Michael DeLong explained, "'Shock and awe' signified focused firepower when we wanted it and where we wanted it. We could bomb a building and leave windows next door unbroken. It was 'shocking' in its precision and 'awesome' in its reliability." In a single 24-hour period,

George W. Bush

Among the hundreds of targets in Baghdad during the "shock and awe" campaign was the presidential palace compound of Saddam Hussein.

more than 1,500 cruise missiles and bombs fell on high-value targets in Baghdad and other Iraqi cities. Television news stations transmitted images of Iraq's burning palaces and government buildings to viewers around the world.

But the airstrikes weren't the only battle scenes of which people had a firsthand view. As the ground war launched on March 20, journalists embedded with various military units reported the action as it happened. The ground assault in the 1991 Persian Gulf War had involved nearly 550,000 coalition troops. But this time, the ground force was made up of fewer than 150,000 soldiers. The smaller force reflected the fact that

POINTING OUT

A DANGEROUS JOB

Although journalists had long covered wars, the Iraq War was the first time news reporters were allowed to join combat units on the battlefield. Through the embed program, journalists participated in basic training. Then they traveled to Iraq to live alongside their assigned units. Reporting on the war was a dangerous job. An estimated 150 journalists and 54 support workers were killed in Iraq between March 2003 and December 2011, according to the Committee to Protect Journalists. At least 117 of the journalists were Iraqi, while 2 were American. The majority of journalists killed during the war died in targeted insurgent attacks rather than combat operations.

Three years after the onset of Operation Iraqi Freedom, the focus of the war had changed, but U.S. troops kept cycling into and out of Iraq via Kuwait.

the Iraqi army was much smaller and weaker than it had been in 1991. In addition, the U.S. had a distinct advantage in terms of weapons, armored vehicles, and communications.

The plan was for the combined American and British forces to make a swift advance on Baghdad from Kuwait. Troops would move in from the north, south, and east to surround the Iraqi capital. Moving under cover of darkness and meeting little resistance at first, U.S. troops made quick progress. When troops did encounter the Iraqi army, the Iraqi fighters often fled. Thousands more surrendered. Even when they did put up a fight, their outdated weapons were little match for American tanks and armored trucks. Within two days, some American units had pushed more than 150 miles (241 km) into Iraq.

But by March 23, U.S. and British soldiers came face-to-face with the *fedayeen* in several cities, including Nasiriyah, Umm Qasr, and Basra. These fighters were not part of the regular army. Instead, they formed a **militia** of fighters willing to die for Hussein. The fedayeen often dressed as civilians and drove civilian cars. Some waved white flags, pretending to surrender. When American forces approached, they opened fire with rocket-propelled grenades, mortars, and assault rifles. Some also carried out suicide attacks, killing U.S. and British troops as well as Iraqi civilians. They also fired on U.S. troops from inside hospitals, schools, and other buildings. They knew U.S. forces would not return fire on such targets.

A three-day sandstorm that began on March 24 provided another challenge. "Even the most technologically sophisticated military was no match for nature," according to embedded CBS correspondent Jim Axelrod.

As American troops encountered suspected fedayeen members, they arrested them if possible and tried to obtain further information.

19

Visibility during the storm was so poor that soldiers had to use GPS units simply to navigate around their camps. Once the storm passed, however, troops again pressed forward. "We weren't marching to Baghdad," said DeLong. "We were sprinting there."

In the north, U.S. forces aided by Kurdish troops took the city of Mosul. Meanwhile, in the south, the British managed to secure the city of Basra. American forces took Nasiriyah and Najaf. By April 2, U.S. forces had secured Karbala, only 65 miles (105 km) from Baghdad.

As U.S. troops closed in on Baghdad, they prepared for the possibility of a chemical attack. Soldiers had been given protective gear, which included heavy suits lined with charcoal, thick vinyl boots and gloves, and gas masks. Commanders expected the Iraqis to make a fierce last stand in Baghdad. But as troops approached Saddam International Airport on the outskirts of the city on April 3, they met little resistance. By that night, they had taken the airport, which they renamed Baghdad International Airport. Meanwhile, the Iraqi information minister, Muhammad Said al-Sahhaf, assured his people that the arrival of American troops in the nation's capital was part of a plan to lure the enemy to defeat.

On April 5, a force of 760 U.S. troops in 30 Abrams tanks and 15 Bradley fighting vehicles

Much of the crowd who witnessed the statue's toppling in Firdos Square was composed of journalists and American troops—Iraqis were largely absent.

carried out the first "thunder run" into Baghdad. Designed to test the city's defenses, the thunder run involved moving at top speed through the city, firing on enemy fighters along the way, without stopping. In little more than 2 hours, the small American force killed 2,000 Iraqi fighters. Only one American was killed in the attack. By the next day, U.S. forces surrounded Baghdad, blocking every possible escape.

A second, larger thunder run on April 7 brought U.S. soldiers to the heart of Baghdad. There they captured Hussein's huge palace complex, even as al-Sahhaf insisted on state TV that there were "no American infidels in Baghdad." By the next day, most of the regime's leaders—including Hussein—had fled. On April 9, the world watched images of American troops helping Iraqi citizens topple a 40-foot-tall (12.2 m) statue of Hussein in downtown Baghdad. The Iraqis dragged the statue's broken head through the streets, spitting at it and slapping it with their shoes. Many Iraqis thanked the U.S. troops for their service. "You have saved us from him," some said. "This is finally justice," an Iraqi man told a reporter.

By April 10, only three weeks after the start of Operation Iraqi Freedom, Baghdad was securely in U.S. control. Over the next few weeks, U.S. and British forces seized control of other Iraqi cities as well. On May 1, Bush landed

President Bush's pronouncement aboard the Abraham Lincoln *was criticized for being premature, as the scope of the mission changed.*

aboard the aircraft carrier USS *Abraham Lincoln*, which had returned to California from service in the Middle East. With a "Mission Accomplished" banner rippling behind him, he told the sailors gathered on deck, "Major combat operations in Iraq have ended. In the battle of Iraq, the United States and our allies have prevailed." The offensive had lasted 43 days. The U.S. had lost 122 soldiers and Britain 33. No one could foresee that the death toll would rise dramatically in the years to come.

POINTING OUT

ABUSE AT ABU GHRAIB

As American troops rounded up Iraqi men they thought might be connected to the insurgency, they sent them to Abu Ghraib, a prison outside Baghdad. In April 2004, pictures of conditions at the prison were publicized on 60 Minutes II. Photographs and reports from soldiers stationed at Abu Ghraib revealed that naked prisoners were handcuffed to doors. Some were forced to wear dogs' leashes and bark while being spit at, urinated on, and beaten. In some cases, prisoners were threatened with electrocution. The scandal sparked rage around the world. Eleven U.S. soldiers were convicted of crimes for their role in the abuse carried out at Abu Ghraib.

CHAPTER THREE

UNSTABLE SITUATION

Officials in the U.S. had hoped that with the fall of Saddam Hussein, the Iraqi people would quickly embrace democracy and establish a new government. But the dictator had brutally repressed all dissent for nearly 30 years. His absence left a power vacuum, with no one stepping forward to take control. In many cities, police officers and security forces abandoned their posts. Chaos descended as looters overtook cities. They broke into government buildings, banks, museums, and even government armories stocked with weapons and ammunition.

In some cases, such looting took place right in front of American troops, who had no orders to stop it. Even when they did try to calm the unruly crowds, the Americans found they did not have enough manpower to control the country of 25 million. As historian Terry Anderson pointed out, "The lawlessness meant that Iraqis' first taste of freedom was chaos. Saddam had been brutal, but at least … had maintained order, prevented violence in the streets, and kept on the water and electricity…. Saddam's certainty and stability had been replaced by American instability and uncertainty."

As the looting continued, Iraqis who had at first cheered the Americans for overthrowing Hussein began to resent their continued presence. As one Iraqi man told a CBS reporter, "Go! We do not like Saddam. But we hate

Hussein fled Baghdad in March 2003 and was arrested nine months later, after U.S. forces discovered his underground hiding place near Tikrit.

The looting of ancient artifacts continued as Iraq's government remained in limbo, and by 2017, security forces were still unearthing objects.

Americans. Leave this place!"

The U.S. established the Coalition Provisional Authority (CPA) to help set up a new Iraqi government. One of the CPA's first acts was to fire all members of the Baath Party, the ruling political party Hussein had controlled. This move left up to 100,000 Iraqis unemployed, since under Hussein, everyone from teachers to government leaders had been required to join the party to get a job. In July, the CPA also dissolved the Iraqi army. This put 400,000 men—most of whom retained their weapons—out of work. According to one

POINTING OUT

LOOTING NATIONAL TREASURES

As chaos descended on Baghdad after the fall of Hussein's regime, looters destroyed thousands of historical treasures. More than 12,000 items stored at Baghdad's National Museum of Antiquities were stolen. Among them were statues, gold and silver necklaces, and pottery from ancient civilizations. Objects too large to be carried away—including a 4,000-year-old clay lion head—were smashed. In addition, looters carried treasures away from Hussein's palaces. One woman who had joined in the looting with her husband and young children said, "I don't feel any guilt at all. We paid for these things a hundred times over. Not a hundred times. A thousand times."

American colonel, this move "was the turning point.... That was it. Every moderate, every person [in Iraq] that had leaned toward us, was furious."

Resentment toward American actions quickly fueled an insurgency, or rebellion. American soldiers found themselves increasingly under attack by snipers and suicide bombers. Insurgents also began to plant improvised explosive devices (IEDs) along roadsides. These explosives were remotely detonated as American vehicles drew close. In addition to targeting U.S. troops, insurgents also took aim at Iraqi citizens and Iraqi officials who were working with the U.S. to get a new government off the ground.

At first, U.S. military leaders struggled to pinpoint those responsible for the insurgency. Some believed the majority of the insurgents were Baathists who remained loyal to Hussein. In an attempt to figure out who was part of the insurgency, U.S. troops forcibly broke into homes. They arrested Iraqi men and subjected them to interrogations. These actions drew even more resentment from the Iraqi people.

On December 14, 2003, American soldiers found Hussein hiding in a tiny underground crawlspace on a farm outside Tikrit. The Iraqi dictator quickly surrendered and was taken into custody. But even his capture—and eventual execution—didn't slow the insurgency.

For many Iraqi people, having foreign soldiers in their communities was perhaps often a source of tension rather than comfort.

Over time, the U.S. came to recognize that the insurgency was not led by a single group. Instead, it was made up of dozens of different factions, including fedayeen, former members of the Iraqi army, and terrorists who had entered the country after Hussein's fall from power. Among the greatest terrorist threats was Abu Musab al-Zarqawi. Al-Zarqawi founded al Qaeda in Iraq, which soon established an even more vicious reputation than its parent organization. Al-Zarqawi frequently kidnapped and killed American and British contractors who had entered Iraq to help with reconstruction projects. He videotaped these killings and posted them on the Internet. Adding to the danger, Iraq seemed to be sinking deeper into a civil war between the country's **Sunni** minority, who had held positions of leadership under Hussein, and the long-oppressed Shiite majority.

Despite the continuing violence, the CPA turned sovereignty over to Iraq on June 28, 2004. In January 2005, Iraqis voted in the country's first free elections. By October, the new Iraqi government had written a constitution. However, the new government was not yet ready to handle its own security. As terror attacks escalated and violence continued between Sunnis and Shiites, U.S. forces remained in place. In addition to fighting insurgents, they also trained the Iraqi army to eventually take

Over the years, weapons such as handheld machine guns from countries such as Russia and the U.S. were sold in Iraq, arming the insurgents.

over security operations.

Meanwhile, a growing antiwar movement was gaining traction in the U.S. In the summer of 2005, Cindy Sheehan grabbed international media attention. Sheehan's 24-year-old son Casey had died in Iraq. She set up a camp on land adjacent to Bush's ranch in Texas. She said she wanted to ask the president "what noble cause" her son had died for. Soon, thousands of protesters from across the country had joined Sheehan at what came to be known as Camp Casey.

Adding to antiwar feelings in the U.S. was

POINTING OUT

DEATH OF A DICTATOR

After being captured in December 2003, Saddam Hussein was interrogated by American officials. He often lectured them on Iraqi history and how his regime fit into Iraq's evolution. When asked about weapons of mass destruction, Saddam revealed that Iraq had ceased its weapons of mass destruction program after the Persian Gulf War. He said he wanted to give the world the impression he still had them to deter threats from neighboring nations such as Iran. After a nine-month trial, Saddam was found guilty of crimes against humanity, including murder, torture, and illegal imprisonment. He was sentenced to death by hanging. On December 30, 2006, that sentence was carried out.

OF THE GULF CO

BRING THE TROOPS HOME NOW!

united for **peac** **stice**
www.unitedforp **org**

BRING THE TR **S HOME** **NOW!**

the fact that a two-year search had failed to find any weapons of mass destruction in Iraq. Some critics asserted the Bush administration had already known Iraq had no such weapons. They said Bush had lied to convince the country to go to war with Hussein. Others thought the Bush administration had genuinely believed Iraq to be a threat. They claimed the decision for war had been based on faulty intelligence. In a 2004 report, the Senate Select Committee on Intelligence concluded that the U.S. intelligence community had overstated the threat Iraq posed, largely because it feared not being able to prevent another 9/11. The next year, the Commission on the Intelligence Capabilities of the United States Regarding Weapons of Mass Destruction issued a more searing report. It declared, "We conclude that the Intelligence Community was dead wrong in almost all of its pre-war judgments about Iraq's weapons of mass destruction. This was a major intelligence failure." The commission said the failure resulted from the use of unreliable human sources as well as poor analysis of existing evidence. The aluminum tubes Iraq had ordered proved to be for conventional rockets, for example, and not for a nuclear program, as officials had assumed.

Still others asserted that the Bush administration had chosen to emphasize certain threats to help make the case for war—despite the uncertainty present in the intelligence gathered. A Senate Intelligence Committee Report concluded that connections the Bush administration had made between Iraq and al Qaeda were "not substantiated by the intelligence." In the case of weapons of mass destruction, the committee reported that the administration failed to communicate the high level of uncertainty regarding the likelihood that Iraq even had such weapons.

CHAPTER FOUR

NEW THREATS

In early 2006, the violence in Iraq intensified as Sunni and Shiite militias launched new waves of attacks against one other. Al Qaeda also continued to direct its terror campaign at both Americans and Iraqis. Hundreds of thousands of Iraqis fled their homes, flooding across the borders of Jordan and Syria. Thousands more Iraqis were killed in the fighting. By June 2006, an average of 100 Iraqi civilians were dying every day in insurgent attacks.

Up until this point, the U.S. military had stuck to conventional warfare methods. Soldiers lived on bases away from the severest fighting. They rolled into cities on tanks to conduct searches, arrest civilians, and shoot at insurgents, then rolled back out once the city had been taken. But by mid-2006, it was clear these methods weren't working. The cities were quickly retaken by insurgents. Plus, American actions only alienated the Iraqi people. They also angered Arab **extremists** in other countries, who poured across Iraq's borders to join al Qaeda's efforts to expel the Americans from Iraq.

But as al Qaeda continued to launch attacks, including against other **Muslims**, a group of Sunni leaders in Anbar Province decided to strike back. They turned from fighting against American troops to fighting alongside them against the terrorists. The Anbar Awakening, as this movement became

In addition to guns, extremists in the Middle East weaponized their beliefs, subverting Islamic texts and teachings to suit their purposes.

35

By July 2007, new strategies to combat the insurgents were bearing fruit in Ramadi—but the city would experience much more strife years later.

known, slowly helped to reduce violence in the province. Still, U.S. military leaders knew this wouldn't be enough to end the insurgency. In January 2007, General **David Petraeus**, commander of the coalition force in Iraq, requested a surge of 20,000 to 30,000 additional U.S. troops. He wanted to launch a counterinsurgency that would make cities safe for local populations and help them set up their own security forces. As part of the counterinsurgency, U.S. troops were trained in Iraqi history and culture. They asked locals about the problems they faced and how they could help. Instead of living

POINTING OUT

THE CRADLE OF CIVILIZATION

*Once known as Mesopotamia, Iraq lies between the Tigris and Euphrates rivers. It was home to many of the world's earliest civilizations, including Sumer, Babylon, and Assyria. Macedonian king Alexander the Great conquered the land in 334 B.C. The Romans later took over and were in turn replaced by the **Ottoman Empire**. The borders of modern Iraq were established when the Ottoman Empire collapsed after World War I. The new country's borders encompassed three distinct groups: Shiite Muslims in the south, Sunni Muslims in the center, and Kurds in the north. Internal clashes among the groups have been common throughout the country's history.*

on remote bases, the soldiers lived in small groups in the cities they were patrolling. They patrolled those cities on foot alongside the Iraqi army, which provided an equal number of troops.

The first months of 2007 proved to be some of the deadliest of the war as the insurgents fought back. But by late summer, security in some Iraqi cities, including Baghdad, had improved. The number of insurgent attacks launched against American and Iraqi forces dropped by more than half.

By the spring of 2008, U.S. casualty levels reached their lowest point since the start of the war. As the situation in Iraq improved, U.S. forces began turning security duties over to the Iraqi army. Contractors poured into the country to begin reconstruction projects. Iraqi families who had fled their homes began to return. People resumed their normal lives. As one journalist reported, "Some shops stay open until late into the evening. Children play in parks, young women stay out after dark, restaurants are filled with families, and old men sit at sidewalk cafes playing backgammon."

On August 31, 2010, U.S. president Barack Obama declared Operation Iraqi Freedom to be over. The final U.S. troops left Iraq in December 2011. The 8-year-long war had cost the U.S. 4,485 soldiers' lives and close to $1 trillion. Some feared that after the U.S. withdrew, Iraq

The American military's lengthy presence in Iraq led to positive outcomes as well, as soldiers connected with locals on a personal level.

would descend back into civil war. Although tensions persisted, the country remained intact. Terrorist groups soon exploited those tensions. Originally part of al Qaeda in Iraq, the newly formed Islamic State of Iraq and the Levant (ISIL)—or the Islamic State—recruited numerous Iraqi Sunnis who resented their reduced role in the Iraqi government. In 2014, ISIL captured the city of Mosul and declared itself an Islamic **caliphate**. The Iraqi army was unable to stop ISIL, which continued its advance. ISIL forces eventually gained control of one-third of Iraq

POINTING OUT

TRYING TO MOVE ON

As they returned home from the Iraq War, many U.S. veterans were angered by the lack of support they found as they struggled to get back to normal life. "There's no way we could have known that we would be used and abused on the battlefield, wounded, traumatized, and then dumped back into society without any counseling or reintegration training," said army specialist Mike Blake. "How could we have known that we would have to fend for ourselves in the job market, without healthcare, with PTSD [post-traumatic stress disorder], with substance abuse, and with trying to reclaim a semblance of the life we had before all this mess started?"

Barack Obama's two terms as president saw his administration's policies shift as the U.S. struggled to handle the conflicts in Iraq.

as well as large portions of eastern Syria. With more than 7 million people under its rule, ISIL enforced strict Islamic law. It promoted jihad, or holy war, against the West. The organization used the Internet to entice thousands of followers from around the world to travel to the Middle East and join its cause.

In August 2014, a U.S.-led coalition of more than 60 countries joined Iraq in military operations against ISIL. The effort lasted three years, but in December 2017, Iraq announced victory over ISIL. In May 2018, the U.S. declared an end to combat operations against ISIL. However, the U.S. said it would maintain troops in the area in case the terrorist organization regrouped.

Although ISIL had lost its hold on physical territory in Iraq and Syria, it still looked to expand its influence over terrorist groups in North Africa, Afghanistan, southeast Asia, and other locations. Many counterterrorism experts also warned that the organization's **ideology** remained firm. Those beliefs inspired a spate of "lone wolf" attacks. Such attacks were planned and carried out without organized support.

Even without the threat of ISIL in its territory, Iraq continued to face serious challenges. Nearly a decade of insurgency, followed by a three-year siege against ISIL, had left much of the country decimated and in need of reconstruction. In

The city of Baghdad, founded in 762, grew into more of a modern metropolis after becoming Iraq's capital in 1920.

addition, a weak economy led to high unemployment and poverty levels. Many Iraqis remained displaced as the fighting ended.

Despite these challenges, in May 2018, Iraqis returned to the polls for democratic elections. Among the 7,000 candidates running for 329 parliamentary seats, the party of Moqtada al-Sadr made a strong showing. During Operation Iraqi Freedom, al-Sadr had led an insurgent group that launched numerous attacks against U.S. forces. Although al-Sadr did not run for office himself, his party's win ensured he would play a large role in choosing the country's next prime minister. This worried some U.S. officials. However, despite his former anti-U.S. stance, al-Sadr said he would honor agreements between Iraq and the U.S.

Despite the questions regarding the future of Iraq, many people acknowledged that a vote for the country's future leader had been unheard of under Saddam Hussein. To some people, that was enough to prove the war in Iraq had been worth it. To others, nothing would ever justify the high cost of the war. As historian Thomas Mockaitis noted, "The final assessment of the war, if indeed there is one, may depend on how Iraq turns out in the long run." And that question is what makes the Iraq War a turning point the world will continue to debate for years to come.

January 16, 1991	A U.S.-led coalition launches Operation Desert Storm; the war ends in Iraqi defeat, and Iraq agrees to submit to UN weapons inspections.
1998	Iraq refuses further weapons inspections, and the U.S. and Britain launch Operation Desert Fox.
September 11, 2001	Al Qaeda operatives crash four planes into the World Trade Center, the Pentagon, and a Pennsylvania field, killing 3,000.
January 29, 2002	In his State of the Union speech, President Bush declares Iraq to be part of an "Axis of Evil," claiming that it has weapons of mass destruction.
October 11, 2002	Congress authorizes Bush to use military force against Iraq.
March 19, 2003	The U.S. launches airstrikes on Baghdad, beginning Operation Iraqi Freedom.
April 3, 2003	U.S. troops take Saddam International Airport in Baghdad.
May 1, 2003	Bush announces the end of major combat operations in Iraq.
July 2003	The CPA dissolves the Iraqi army, leading to resentment that starts an insurgency.
December 14, 2003	Saddam Hussein is captured near Tikrit; in 2006, he is executed for crimes against humanity.
June 28, 2004	The U.S. turns sovereignty over to Iraq.
January 2005	The Iraqi people vote in their first free election in more than 50 years.
January 2007	A surge of more than 20,000 U.S. troops arrives in Iraq to help with counterinsurgency operations.
August 31, 2010	President Obama announces that Operation Iraqi Freedom is over; the final U.S. troops leave Iraq in December 2011.
2014	A new terrorist organization, ISIL, takes over large parts of Iraq and Syria and declares itself a caliphate.
December 2017	Iraq declares victory over ISIL.
May 2018	The party of former insurgent Moqtada al-Sadr makes a strong showing in Iraqi elections.

al Qaeda—the terrorist network founded by Saudi Arabian Osama bin Laden in the 1980s; the organization seeks jihad, or holy war, against the U.S. and the West and works to institute Islamic governments around the world

Baath Party—political party formed in Syria in the 1940s to promote Arab unity, secular government, and state control of industry and the economy; the Baath Party held power in Iraq from 1963 until Hussein's overthrow in 2003

caliphate—the chief Muslim civil and religious leader

centrifuges—machines that spin materials to separate them into their component parts; nuclear centrifuges are used to prepare uranium for use in nuclear weapons and nuclear power plants

David Petraeus—U.S. general who served as commander of forces in Iraq from 2007 to 2008 and was responsible for developing key counterinsurgency tactics; Petraeus later served as commander of U.S. Central Command and commander of the International Security Assistance Force in Afghanistan before becoming director of the CIA for a short time

dictator—a ruler with complete power, who often rules by force

drones—unmanned aircraft operated by remote control or computers; some drones carry video equipment or missiles

extremists—people who believe in using violence or other extreme measures to enforce uncompromising views

ideology—set of ideas and beliefs followed by an individual or group

Kurds—members of an ethnic group living in parts of Iran, Iraq, Syria, and Turkey, most of whom are Sunni Muslims and speak a language related to Persian

militia—groups of citizens who band together to form their own army, often to fight the government

Muslims—followers of Islam, a religion that says there is one God—Allah—and that Muhammad is his prophet

Ottoman Empire—an empire that ruled over much of southeastern Europe, the Middle East, and North Africa from the 1300s until 1922

preemptive—describing something that is done as a preventive measure

regimes—rules of specific governments or leaders, usually oppressive

sanctions—measures (such as trade bans) taken by the UN or by individual nations against a country that has violated international law to convince it to end the violation

Shiite—members of a branch of Islam that believes Ali, the son-in-law of the prophet Muhammad, is the rightful successor to the prophet; about one-tenth of the world's Muslim population belongs to the Shiite branch

Sunni—members of a traditionalist branch of Islam that recognizes the first four caliphs, or Muslim rulers, as Muhammad's successors; the majority of Muslims belong to the Sunni branch

Taliban—a militant, conservative Islamic movement in Afghanistan that enforced harsh laws, such as excluding women from public life

Anderson, Terry. *Bush's Wars.* New York: Oxford University Press, 2011.

DeLong, Michael. *Inside CENTCOM: The Unvarnished Truth about the Wars in Afghanistan and Iraq.* Washington, D.C.: Regnery, 2004.

Mockaitis, Thomas, ed. *The Iraq War Encyclopedia.* Santa Barbara, Calif.: ABC-CLIO, 2013.

Nixon, John. *Debriefing the President: The Interrogation of Saddam Hussein.* New York: Blue Rider Press, 2016.

Purdum, Todd. *A Time of Our Choosing: America's War in Iraq.* New York: Henry Holt, 2003.

Rather, Dan. *America at War: The Battle for Iraq; a View from the Frontlines.* New York: Simon & Schuster, 2003.

Seftel, Bennett. "Threat Report 2018: ISIS in the Spotlight." *The Cipher Brief.* May 14, 2018. https://www.thecipherbrief.com/threat-report-2018-isis -spotlight.

Sifry, Micah, and Christopher Cerf, eds. *The Iraq War Reader: History, Documents, Opinions.* New York: Touchstone, 2003.

Council on Foreign Relations: The Iraq War
https://www.cfr.org/timeline/iraq-war
Browse an interactive timeline of significant events during the Iraq War.

TIME: Seven Years in Iraq: An Iraq War Timeline
http://content.time.com/time/specials/packages/0,28757,1967340,00.html
This site offers photos, videos, and explanations of the various phases of the
Iraq War.

Note: Every effort has been made to ensure that the websites listed above are suitable for children, that they have educational value, and that they contain no inappropriate material. However, because of the nature of the Internet, it is impossible to guarantee that these sites will remain active indefinitely or that their contents will not be altered.